BRIGHT DAWN

BRIGHT DAWN

Discovering Your
Everyday Spirituality

By
S. K. Kubose

Published by
Dharma House
8334 Harding Ave.
Skokie, IL 60076

Cover photograph by Linda Barrett
Cover design by Lisa Nakamoto

First Edition. 2004
Printed in the United States of America

LCCN: 2003093977
ISBN: 0-9642992-1-6

ORDERING INFORMATION
Online Orders: www.brightdawn.org
Telephone Orders 24/7: (800) 247-6553
Autographed Copies: see page 151

To My Parents
Rev. Gyomay & Minnie Kubose
My Spiritual Source

CONTENTS

In Gratitude 11

Foreword 15

Introduction 19

Darkness 25

Bathroom 31

Shoes 39

Driving 47

Sky 63

Water 73

Running 79

Keep Going 103

Bridge to Inspiration Point 115

Bright Dawn 127

Epilogue 137

Map 143

Additional Information 145

Bright Dawn

IN GRATITUDE

Many people have influenced my life and have been a part of the broad interdependency that led to this book becoming a reality. My late parents were a very powerful spiritual influence. My family and relatives have provided constant unconditional support and encouragement: my late grandparents Tsuneshichi and Taka Taniguchi; my uncles and aunts Kay and Alyce Taniguchi; George and

Amy Taniguchi; my cousins and their families: Bruce, Aimy, and Bethany Wilbur; Earl Taniguchi; Glenn, Royce, and Brandon Taniguchi; Dana and Stacy Taniguchi; Glenn, Jill, Blair, and Brooks Iwamoto; and Susan and Joy Taniguchi.

My brother Don Kubose and sister Joyce Prosise are like two pillars holding me up. Their respective spouses, Joyce Kubose and Robert Prosise, are what hold them up, including the extended Prosise, Okamura, and Ishikawa relatives. My niece Shauna has been like a spark plug in the engine of my car. Her husband Richardson Fleuridor provides her gasoline. I want to acknowledge Kristine Kubose Perry and her daughters Marika and Karissa; Darren and Tina Kubose and their children Kamryn, Emiko, and Trevor; and Gallegos relatives.

I am grateful for a very solid in-law network: Henry and Michi Kimura, Yuji and Eimi Okano, Tad and Naomi Asano; including the extended Okano, Asano, Shimazaki, and Herlinger relatives. I give thanks to the Nakao, Nagata, and Muramoto families; plus the Armstrong, Robinson, Smelser, Yamada, and Yoshimura relatives.

The support and encouragement of people such as Elizabeth Bahe, Maryann Brandon, Paul and Tonko Doi, Philip Goff, Asayo Horibe, George and Ritsuko Inouye, Nancy Schaffner, Haruko

Tanaka, Yoshi Tanaka, David Toguri, the Yu family, and many others have helped further my efforts for the Kubose Dharma Legacy organization that supports my life work.

I have been nourished by friends from the Heartland Sangha, the Japanese American, Buddhist, and interfaith communities in the Chicago area; personal friends from Ray School, Hyde Park High School, the Vikings, plus friends from my years in California, Iowa, North Carolina, Wisconsin, and Japan.

I acknowledge Dharma friends all over North and South America, Canada, Europe, and Asia. I shout "Mahalo" across the Pacific Ocean to the Hawaii Sanghas.

I have been privileged to share the manuscript draft of the book with colleagues and friends who have provided valuable advice and support: Dr. Alfred Bloom, Richard Zenyo Brandon, Dharmavidya David Brazier, Cynthia Brooke, Rev. Marvin Harada, Dr. Victor Sogen Hori, Robert Leopold, Janet Lipner, Rev. Bob Oshita, Elizabeth Plotnick, Ruth Tabrah, Dr. Ken Tanaka, Rev. Robert Thompson, Eddie Toppel, Dr. Taitetsu Unno, Rev. Tetsuo Unno, and Wayne Yokoyama.

I express thanks to special friends who have helped significantly to shape the book: Gordon Bermant, Keith Cunningham, Brian

Nagata, Numata Center staff, and Sam Shapiro. I gratefully acknowledge Linda Barrett, talented artist with a camera, for the cover and author photographs. I appreciate Tod Tatsui's technical graphic arts assistance. I sincerely thank Lisa Nakamoto who designed the cover of the book and assisted in the book's production, you are the best!

I acknowledge my sons Kanon and Tate, who are a part of me, and embrace Tate's wife, Denise, a terrific daughter-in-law, who has joined our family. To my wife Adrienne, you are truly my "better half." Anyone who knows the two of us, knows this is true.

FOREWORD

Buddhism has been practiced in America for over a century, but it was Rev. Gyomay Kubose, the author's father, who had the vision to emphasize a Buddhist approach that is easily accessible to Americans. In 1944 he founded a non-sectarian Buddhist temple in Chicago that had a new direction. Dogma was discarded for an innovative, non-dualistic approach, the "Way of Oneness."

It is an interesting time to be a Buddhist in America. Rev. Koyo, and his father before him, have outlined a path of practice that is both rewarding and inspiring. They have shared the teachings of the Way of Oneness and a non-dualistic approach with several generations of Buddhists, changing the face of Buddhism in Chicago, and perhaps in America.

"Bright Dawn: Discovering Your Everyday Spirituality" by Rev. Koyo Kubose, carries on his father's mission to establish a distinctly American Buddhism that can be practiced in everyday life. This book offers the life-changing lessons of learning to take a wide view, to keep going, and to find spirituality in the mindful practice of being "one" with nature. Rev. Koyo writes, "The suchness (naturalness) of nature provides simple but deep teachings."

The book begins as Rev. Koyo awakens to a new day. We experience his grateful awareness as he prepares for a morning run. We accompany him as he arrives at the running path along Lake Michigan, before the sun rises. As he runs along the path, he presents ideas of gratitude and perseverance that inspire the reader. Rev. Koyo presents his experience of watching the sunrise and relates it to universal teachings for everyday living and seeing what is around him with awareness. In the book, he demonstrates how to find one's own light with clear direction. He show us how to let go of our narrow egocentric view and open up to a broader view of ourselves in the world.

Rev. Koyo invites us to look mindfully at our daily life. He shares ways for us to experience this mindfulness practice so we may discover our own spiritual path and to incorporate spirituality into everyday life.

Cynthia Brooke, President
Heartland Sangha

Bright Dawn

INTRODUCTION

Like many people, I run for health and for recreational sport. Over the years, the motivation and meaning behind my running have evolved in different ways. When I started running along the lakefront, running included appreciating the beauty of nature. Early morning running and seeing the sunrise became full of spiritual significance after my father's death about three years ago.

My father, Rev. Gyomay M. Kubose, was a Buddhist minister. His Buddhist Name, Gyomay, means "Bright Dawn." The whole activity of getting up early, running at the lakefront, and seeing the dawn is a mini-pilgrimage that starts my day. This way of greeting each day is an important part of my daily spiritual practice.

The purpose of my writing is to encourage individual spirituality by sharing how teachings can be discovered within everyday activities. Such teachings can be integrated with and enhance traditional religious approaches or they can stand alone as a general kind of humanistic spirituality. Of course, spiritual experiences can occur within a traditional religious context but spirituality is fundamentally a private, personal experience beyond beliefs and concepts.

Some people may feel that their religious identity is strictly bound by a particular set of religious rituals. Such people may be conditioned to believe that they are not allowed to engage in any practices that are not explicitly specified as part of their religion. They may feel that other practices are not only prohibited but are dangerous. Religions need to take the lead in nurturing inter-religious harmony. Interfaith dialogue is a beginning toward mutual respect and understanding.

In addition, we need to give people permission (those who feel they need such permission) to broaden their spiritual horizons without feeling they are violating their own religious tradition. Individuals can be empowered to explore and discover new ways of how the sacred is expressed in the secular. In other words, it is okay to find personalized teachings that come out of one's own life situations. It is okay to create and use customized daily spiritual rituals in addition to traditional religious rituals. It is okay to adapt practices from any religious tradition and make them relevant to one's own spirituality.

In America there is freedom *of* religion, and as the atheists remind us, freedom *from* religion. We also need to have freedom *within* a religion. A religion needs to be flexible and creative in order to meet the needs of different individuals. How wonderful if a religion could be so "alive" and open that it could encourage spirituality in a wide variety of ways. In Buddhism it is said there are 84,000 paths up the mountain.

The Way of Oneness does not mean that all become one and the same. In fact, it means quite the opposite. Oneness means the recognition of differences. This provides the basis for harmony. There is harmony when each person is recognized as unique and absolute. In knowing one's own uniqueness, there is untold respect for others' uniqueness. Only when one respects oneself, can he or she really respect others. Each person should be the finest that he or she is— without comparison to others.

The vision of oneness is seen in the reflection of many. The United States was founded on the principle of *E Pluribus Unum* (out of many, one). America is still a country of immigrants. Our nation is a wonderful "salad bowl" of different ethnic, racial, and religious backgrounds.

The abundance of religious pluralism in America calls for mutual understanding. Every individual's spiritual path should be respected. Religious teachings point to spiritual truths but each individual has to bring those truths into one's own life. As each individual's life is unique, so is his or her spiritual life. This is how I view my own spirituality and is what I have shared by relating various teachings to my daily ritual of lakefront running and seeing the sunrise.

The description of the running path along Lake Michigan is factual. I have included photographs and a map. Anyone is welcome to run or walk the route that I describe. However, the main purpose of this book is to encourage readers to find teachings in their own activities no matter where they live.

Our physical health is maintained by daily hygiene practices like brushing teeth and washing up. It is no less important to maintain our spiritual health by daily mindfulness practices. It is through individual spirituality that we can contribute to society and the times we live in. Each of us can make a contribution to a culture of values that encourage living with wisdom and compassion. In oneness, may it be so.

S. K. Kubose

Bright Dawn

DARKNESS

My bedroom is still dark. The edges of the window curtain are dimly illuminated by light from the street. It is quiet in the special way that an early morning is quiet. A one-eyed glance towards the head board... the clock's red numbers glow 5:15 A.M. I lie in that not-quite-awake, not-quite-asleep state.

In the dark room, a thought comes floating through my mind, "Spiritual journeys always start in the darkness." I recall a saying, "In a dark time, the eye begins to see." Just as the physical eye opens wider in the dark, "wisdom's eye" begins to open under the adversity of hard times. Remembering the depression of my youth when I felt the heavy meaninglessness of life, there were many mornings when I thought, "Why get out of bed; is there anything to look forward to today?" Everything paled next to the deep darkness of my own existential abyss.

Trying to climb out from the bottom of a dark abyss is a daunting task. In Buddhist literature there's a story of a worm trapped inside a tall bamboo stalk. The worm climbs upward but encounters a solid joint in the bamboo stalk. He eats his way through and continues to climb upward. There seems to be no other way to freedom than to continue climbing upward, eating his way through the many joints in the stalk. As strong and determined as the worm is, the bamboo stalk is very tall and there's still a long way to go. The worm gets tired and has to rest in the darkness. For the first time, he notices a small light coming through a tiny crack in the wall of the bamboo. He chews though the side of the bamboo and in an instant, he is free!

One part of this story has to do with darkness. The presence of darkness is so obvious that it usually would not be emphasized; but actually it is the darkness that enables the worm to notice the small ray of light. In applying the story to spirituality, a spiritual journey can be expressed as moving from darkness towards light; that is, from ignorance to wisdom. Although light or wisdom is important, darkness or ignorance is also important. The first step towards wisdom is to realize that one is ignorant. Thus, wisdom is not separate from ignorance; the two are intimately connected. Stars are seen because the night sky is dark. Not only that but as the sky gets darker, even more stars can be seen.

The spiritual journey is to look deeper and deeper within oneself. Realizing the darkness within oneself is the beginning of one's enlightenment. Each of us has "dark" qualities that may not be obvious. It is not so much that we hide these qualities from others but that we are not fully aware of them ourselves. Spiritual growth requires the prerequisite of introspection. We need to look carefully, and honestly examine our own basic ignorance, greed, anger, and other aspects of ourselves that we rarely see clearly. Looking within is the key. The journey begins in the darkness.

Another story comes to my mind, as I lie in the darkness of my bedroom. A man was walking home at night and lost the key to his front door. He stood on his front porch and began to look around for his lost key. A friend happened by and helped him look all over the porch without success. The friend asked, "Can you remember approximately where you lost the key?" The man said, "It was probably on the walk leading up to my front porch." The friend exclaimed, "Then why were you looking on the porch?!" The man replied, "Well, the light is better here." The moral is that if the key is in the darkness, then one has to go into the darkness to find it.

Actually, it is not so much that the key is in the darkness, but rather that the darkness itself is the key. Darkness is crucial to the existence and meaning of light. Darkness can be likened to the mud at the bottom of a pond. It is often said that the lotus, the Buddhist flower, only grows in a muddy pond. The lotus rises above the mud and surface of the pond to blossom beautifully. Spiritually, the muddy pond refers to the "mud" within oneself. It's not easy for sunlight to penetrate down to this kind of inner mud. Yet, the roots of the lotus are firmly in the mud and receive nourishment from the mud. The lotus cannot live without the mud. The beautiful blossom seen above the surface of the water is intimately connected to the mud below.

As human beings, it is impossible to get rid of our dark, muddy qualities such as anger, greed and ignorance. We can never get rid of egotistic self-centeredness; it is part of life's energy and what it means to be a human being. However, when we become aware of the suffering caused by a self-centered perspective, change becomes possible and a broader perspective is revealed. Difficulties and suffering are not eliminated, but one can learn to deal with them wisely. Tragic events and personal suffering, although undesired, are what enable the cultivation of wisdom.

Wisdom is symbolized by light. Light enables us to see truth, reality as it is. Truth, in Buddhism, is called Dharma. Spiritual truth is to live in the light (wisdom) of the Dharma. As a seed buried in the earth grows up towards the sun, and as the leaves of a plant always face the light, I find myself always turning towards the truth of the Dharma. I too want to face the sun. It is time to start the day. My bedroom clock now reads 5:37 A.M.

Bright Dawn

BATHROOM

I make my way to the bathroom. This morning, like most mornings, I prepare to go running and watch the sunrise at the lakefront. I glance out of the bathroom window at the branches of the trees lining the street. Everything is calm, not much wind. I nod and smile. I sit down on the toilet and do my "Toilet Gassho." Gassho is a Japanese Buddhist term referring to the act of putting the palms of one's hands together in respect and gratitude. I sure am thankful my inner plumbing is working.

Giving thanks before eating is a common practice but we should also be thankful for the important excretion process. Elimination of toxic waste products resulting from digestion of food is crucial in maintaining life. I want to extend my gratitude awareness to different aspects of daily living. I have established Toilet Gassho as an everyday spiritual practice. Instead of doing a traditional two-handed Gassho, I often put up one hand in front of my chest for an informal Gassho. Other times I just like to bow my head, and this triggers the mindful awareness that is the essence of Gassho.

The privacy of a bathroom is a great place for quiet reflection. It occurs to me that not only do we need to flush out bodily waste products for good health, but we also should get rid of the *mental* waste products that invariably accumulate in the course of daily interactions with others. Why poison oneself by hanging on to such toxic things as self-pity, guilt, envy, and resentments. By doing morning Toilet Gassho we can empty ourselves out mentally and start a fresh new day. The Buddha taught how to let go and not be hurt by verbal abuse, blame and criticism. To me, BM can also stand for "Buddha Movement."

This morning I happen to be wearing a T-shirt that I received as a gift a few years ago. Written on the front of the T-shirt is a concise comparison of the basic philosophies of the world's religions. The analysis uses the theme of "Shit Happens" which is taken from a popular bumper sticker. A mental association sidetracks me and I visualize a bumper sticker on a Zen meditator's car that reads, "Sit Happens."

Then I remember another cartoon where the CEO of a fertilizer company is explaining to a group of visitors, "Our manufacturing process has 25 stages, each monitored by stringent quality control procedures before our product is packaged and distributed all over the world. So, contrary to popular opinion, it doesn't just happen."

Enough of my mental associations, back to the comparative analysis of the philosophies of the world religions. For a humorous piece of work the analysis is not bad. For example,

Hinduism: This shit happened before.
Catholic: If shit happens, you deserved it.
Judaism: Why does shit always happen to *us*?
Buddhism: When shit happens, it's not really shit.

What does the saying about Buddhism mean? It means that what is considered a bad thing often can be a blessing in disguise. Spiritual growth often results from painful events. This doesn't mean we should seek out tragedies. Regardless of what we want or don't want, life will bring all kinds of experiences to us. A great lesson in life is learning how to make use of suffering; that is, how to suffer wisely. The Buddhist response to tragedy is to cultivate wisdom.

In the spiritual world it is said, "Misfortune is fortune." People who experience mainly good fortune have a hard time appreciating what they have. They also have difficulty feeling any real empathy with the misfortune of others. A lack of appreciation and compassion can make for a very shallow, superficial life. On the other hand, misfortune and personal tragedy can mold one's character in life-changing ways. In other words, "When shit happens, it's not really shit."

Quotes from existential philosophers come to mind, like Camus' "In the midst of winter, I discovered within myself an invincible summer" and Sartre's "Life begins on the other side of despair." Other philosophical sayings begin flooding my thoughts. To counter this over-intellectualizing, I recall Gestalt therapist, Fritz Perls, who outlined three kinds of verbal "shit" that are detrimental to concretely experiencing reality and authentically encountering others. The first kind of shit he calls "Chicken-shit" which refers to meaningless social verbiage like, "Hello, how are you?" or "How's everything going?" The second, bigger kind of shit is the common "Bull-shit" in which we give rationalizations and excuses instead of expressing the simple truth of things. The biggest kind of verbal shit we engage in can be called "Elephant-shit." This is when we over-philosophize or over-psychologize and make things too abstract and removed from actual life. When these kinds of shit pile up too much, everything starts to stink and we need to flush them down the proverbial toilet. Whenever I catch myself "over-thinking" while sitting on the toilet, I say to myself, "Flush!"

Many kinds of lessons can be learned in the bathroom. After washing up at the bathroom sink, I squeeze toothpaste onto my toothbrush. As I brush my teeth, I like to think that I am also cleaning out potential "mean-spirited" words from my mouth. This is a reminder to be mindful of how I talk to others during the coming day. I want to be patient and understanding, especially with members of my own family.

There was a newspaper comic strip called Dave. In one strip there were four panels. The first panel shows Dave flossing his teeth in the bathroom; his wife is calling him from the hall-way, "Dave!?" The second panel shows Dave still flossing and not responding to his wife, who continues to call, "Dave!?" In the third panel Dave yells, "What!? Go away! Leave me alone!" The last panel shows the wife, Darla, in the bathroom glaring at Dave. With floss still hanging out of his mouth, Dave is pointing to his mouth, saying, "Look Darla, I'm sorry! I was cleaning it and it accidentally went off!"

The mouth, indeed, is like a loaded gun. We should treat our mouths as carefully as a dangerous weapon. Some of us shoot off our mouths as though they had hair triggers. It seems like whizzing all around us are bullets of insults and the exploding shrapnel of criticism and blame. Some people have mouths like a 357 magnum and they carry extra ammo clips. Whoa, there's a 12-gauge shotgun over there! Harsh words injure people and can cause deep wounds. We often criticize others in the name of honesty when actually our harsh words reflect our own inner problems and insecurities.

The Dalai Lama has said, "Kindness is my religion." Basic truths in life are simple but hard to put into practice. A disciple asked his teacher, "What is Buddhism?" The teacher replied, "Be kind; do not harm others." The disciple said, "Even a two-year old child knows that!" "Yes," the teacher said, "but not many adults can live accordingly." It is easy to let our values decay if we don't live them.

I recall a cartoon of a person moving a piece of floss back and forth between his ears. A box next to him was labeled, "Mental Floss." The caption said, "Want to prevent truth decay? Use mental floss everyday— to dislodge hardened expectations and putrefying cynicism."

As I finish up in the bathroom, I think about how my morning hygiene routine has become part of a daily spiritual practice. I like that. The bathroom's cozy privacy brings out intimate conversations that one can have with oneself. The bathroom can be a very powerful sacred space.

Bright Dawn

SHOES

Leaving the bathroom, I put on my running clothes and shoes. I have a ritual of mindfully lacing up my shoes. I like the snug feeling of putting my feet into my comfortable running shoes and pulling the laces tight. This makes me feel that all is right with the world.

A basketball player said his coach, the legendary John Wooden, taught him many things, even how to tie his shoelaces before a game. It was this kind of attention to detail that mentally prepared players to perform their best. Yet, it's more than just getting ready for action. Mindfully doing something contains a mystery beyond the physical doing. In Buddhism, this "mystery" is called the "suchness" of things.

In the case of shoes, the suchness includes a quiet but dynamic quality. Shoes enable a person to get around. Shoes can signify traveling or going on a trip. Shoes can symbolize one's life journey. Shunryu Suzuki, founder of the San Francisco Zen Center, was a pioneering Zen teacher in America. At his funeral, Suzuki Roshi's wife wore his straw sandals during the procession to the cemetery.

A more mundane but personal example is when I got married wearing my father's shoes. This was not planned. The week before my wedding I bought a new pair of dress shoes during my lunch break at work. On my wedding day, I opened the shoebox and to my surprise, the box contained an old pair of junky shoes! My co-workers had played a trick on me. There was no time to remedy the situation so I borrowed my father's shoes. I don't know what influence this had on my marriage but my parents were married for 64 years and as of this writing, my wife and I have been together for 36 years.

It took about 17 years after my wedding for me to follow in my father's footsteps and to join him on the ministerial staff at the temple he had established some 40 years earlier. In my youth and even well into my 30's I had never really considered going into the ministry. Although my father was a prominent minister, he never tried to influence me toward his calling. Still, it is not uncommon for ministers' sons to also become ministers. Other Buddhist ministers and I would jokingly lament that we didn't end up in lucrative professions because we had the "bad" karma of being born into a minister's family. When someone asked, "Why did you become a minister?" The simple reply was, "Bad karma." This is a minister's joke. I love my profession. It is very gratifying to follow in the Buddha's and my father's footsteps.

Shoes can concretely signify a role model's inspirational life. Oprah Winfrey has a television talk show in Chicago. She rose from humble beginnings to become very successful. On one show, she was interviewing people in the audience about what inspired them in life. A woman stood up and started telling how she had bought a pair of Oprah's shoes. Oprah explained that some of her wardrobe had been auctioned off for a charity cause. The woman said she bought the shoes even though she wore size 7 while Oprah's shoes were of a different size. Oprah spoke up, "I'm a size 10." The woman nodded and continued, "Whenever I got discouraged with how my life was going, I would take Oprah's shoes out of my closet and I would... I would..." The woman was having difficulty articulating herself because of her emotions. Oprah said, "You would stand in my shoes." "That's right, I would stand in your shoes and get the courage to keep going." Both women had tears in their eyes.

Shoes not only symbolize one's life journey but shoes literally make it possible to make that journey. Shoes protect our feet. I always try to respect my shoes. Some people take off their shoes and casually throw them around. I line up my shoes neatly side by side.

My father was famous for telling generations of Sunday school children, "When you take off your shoes, thank them. Your shoes protected your feet all day, never complaining." He would tell the children to pat their shoes and say, "Thank you my little shoes."

When some of these children grew up and came back to visit my father's temple, they would often mention this teaching of thanking their shoes. One young man told how he was thinking about this teaching when he was in basic training after being drafted into the army. He was sitting on his bunk bed, shining his boots, when a soldier in the next bunk yelled, "Hey, this guy is talking to his shoes!" Another man dying of cancer told me, "One thing in my life that I'm grateful for is that I met your father 40 years ago... and yes, I am also grateful for my shoes."

One wouldn't think that such a simple teaching like thanking one's shoes would have such a profound effect on people. Gratitude for such little things shows how intimate relationships are possible through mindful awareness. I know a runner who just can't throw away his old shoes. In his car trunk are dozens of old running shoes. His shoes are like old friends to him. Another runner periodically conducts a "Gratitude Service" for his old shoes before he donates them away. Services like this for things used in daily living are common in the East.

For example, once a year, the seamstresses in Japan gather all their broken needles, and have a service to express their gratitude. Needles are crucial to the livelihood of a seamstress. Broken needles are not casually discarded or taken for granted. Gratitude Services deepen awareness of our interdependency with not just other people but with inanimate objects. This opens up a new level of respect and communication.

I pause to bend down and pat my shoes. I see details in the designs on my shoes as if for the first time. Patting my shoes in gratitude before going out for a run is a spiritual practice for me. Being grateful to one's shoes or to some other particular thing always goes beyond whatever one is being thankful for. One becomes more aware of being grateful in general; one becomes a grateful person.

Some people like to think they accomplish things on their own. "Nobody gave me anything. I earned everything I've gotten." Maybe such people think that to be grateful is to show dependence and weakness. Egotistic persons who feel they can control and make things go their way are usually clever and skillful. Yet, such people also become good at blaming and rationalizing because things do not go one's way all the time. Sooner or later, arrogance and self-deception take their toll, on both the body and the mind.

The psychologist, Carl Jung, stated, "All mental illness has a spiritual cause." Someone else said, "I have never seen a grateful person become mentally ill." Gratefulness and mental problems don't go together. Of course, one has to be sincere. If a person superficially expresses

gratefulness just for self-centered motives, everything will become ugly.

It has been said that the only two things in life
one needs to remember are, "Always be sincere…
and don't forget to laugh." I pat my shoes mindfully to avoid it becoming a mechanical ritual.
Then with a smile and quiet chuckle, my shoes
and I are ready to roll!

Bright Dawn

DRIVING

I am now ready to leave my house. I live in Skokie, a suburb just north of Chicago. Lake Michigan is about three miles east from my house. If I were a real runner, I'd run to the lake, but I drive. I get into my van, which has license plates that read, "BRTDAWN." I quietly sit behind the steering wheel for a moment. Then I do what I call "doing the wheel." With one hand I trace along the outline of the steering wheel, followed by four strokes in the air cutting across the wheel. First diagonally left to right, then diagonally right to left, then horizontally across the center, and lastly a vertical stroke down the middle. These four strokes make an imaginary 8-spoked wheel. This pattern of hand movements is my own invention. I consider this a Dharma Wheel, which is the symbol for Buddhism, just as the cross is the symbol for Christianity and the Star of David is for Judaism.

"Doing the wheel" using my car's steering wheel is how I evoke a calm feeling before driving off. It is a reminder to drive mindfully. I try to use the car as a special meditation space and use driving to practice tranquil courtesy. Although the

act of driving is basically automatic, I try to stay centered and not allow other drivers to disrupt my serenity. To get upset at rude drivers is giving them power over me. Instead, rude drivers can be considered teachers in disguise. They give me the opportunity to learn patience. Yes, I know, sometimes there are too many "teachers" out there!

Fortunately, traffic is light during my early morning drive to the lake. As I head east on Main Street, I enter Evanston, a neighboring suburb. At Chicago Avenue I go one block north to Lee Street, turn right and head east towards the lake. I take the same route every time I go to the lake. The route is so familiar that it's easy to become inattentive. Once I almost hit a pedestrian while turning at an intersection. Many accidents happen at intersections. It occurs to me that interpersonal interactions are like street intersections. Both are places or times when two people and two lives pass by each other. Our daily lives contain many routine moments of dealing with other people. Careless, insensitive words can have long lasting effects on people's lives.

Worse than being careless, one could react in anger. There was an incident in the news of a driver who hit a bicycle rider. Earlier they had almost collided, and they yelled at each other. The driver, in a flash of anger, stomped on the gas pedal. The bicyclist was killed. A jury found the driver guilty of first-degree murder and he was sentenced to 45 years in prison. A routine driving incident, a split-second angry reaction, two lives and two families profoundly affected.

Seemingly small or quick reactions can have big consequences. I try not to take my routine interactions with others lightly. Each interaction with someone, be it a store clerk or a family member, is like a crossroads where one can mindfully make a decision to be fully present.

By using driving as a mindfulness practice, I find myself becoming a more mindful person. I start to become more aware of how I interact with others. I can make any interaction into a genuine encounter full of positive impact. I become aware that each moment is a unique, absolute moment; a precious moment not to be wasted. It has been said that each moment is a gift, and that is why this moment is called the present.

It is easy to take the present moment for granted… especially when driving because one is usually in a hurry to get someplace. Do you know any driver who wishes the traffic light ahead to turn red? Not likely… instead, everybody speeds up to beat a red light. Here's a good mind-fulness practice: whenever you're stopped at a red light, take a deep breath and say, "Ah... what a great opportunity to pause and refresh myself."

Somehow driving a car often makes us feel like we should hurry up. And woe to any idiot who gets in our way! We compulsively want to find the quickest route to get where we're going. We are obsessed with time and efficiency. I heard a story of a city slicker who was driving in the country and saw a farmer under an apple tree, surrounded by pigs. The farmer was lifting up pig after pig so each could eat its fill of apples from the branches. The city slicker shouted, "It'd be a lot faster if you just shook the tree!" The farmer smiled and in a slow drawl replied, "What's time to a pig?"

When driving, I have discovered the serenity of hitting the brakes and slowing down. Try it and see how you feel. I remember a cartoon showing a traffic sign that said, "Spiritual Zone... Speed Limit Zero." When the tail lights of a car in front of you blink red, you can imagine the lights are the Buddha's eyes... making his spiritual presence known to you.

A Shin Buddhist minister shared an experi-ence he had while driving in New York City. In

Shin Buddhism, Amida Buddha is of central importance. Amida can be said to symbolize perfect wisdom and infinite compassion. By coincidence, there is a company called Amida that makes traffic control signs. When road construction requires traffic to merge from two lanes into one lane, a large sign with a blinking arrow directs the traffic flow. Sometimes there is a sticker on the sign that reads "Amida." The Shin Buddhist

minister had an epiphany when he saw such a sign. He was driving in rush-hour traffic, feeling quite stressed. Approaching the sign, he was surprised to see the "Amida" sticker. This relaxed him and after that he never got stressed while driving. In fact, this experience slowed his whole life down and transformed his perspective on the pace of his life. Through awareness in our everyday activities, any moment can become full of personal significance.

Slowing down has another application. We slow down so that we can stop. Being able to stop is important in life. It is important when we want to stop certain ways of behaving. Seeing a stop sign while driving can remind us to develop our internal "stopping power." We need "stopping power" to change behavior because some behaviors are difficult to stop doing.

For example, it is difficult to change eating habits. Some years ago, a Buddhist minister was visiting the Chicago stockyards. He saw cows being forced down a narrow gangway. He saw the fear in their eyes as a man with a heavy sledgehammer killed each one with a blow to the head. The minister cringed hearing the scream of pigs as they were hoisted up and their jugular veins cut open. Blood was everywhere. The minister vowed he would never eat meat again. At the end of the tour, he was in a room with spotless white walls. Shelves were filled with row after row of packages of all kinds of meat. The minister's first thought was, "Hey, maybe I can get a good deal here." The minister related his experience to demonstrate how easily good intentions can fall victim to selfish desires.

It is difficult to say "stop" to life-styles that perpetuate suffering for ourselves and others. It is difficult to challenge our way of living because often we are conditioned and manipulated by vested social and economic interests. We feel swept along by large forces seemingly beyond our control. We cannot say, "Stop the world; I want to get off!" Both the just and the unjust, the good and the bad are subject to the conditions of the time.

There is an account in the Buddhist literature of Angulimala, a criminal who lived during Gautama Buddha's time. Angulimala was a feared highwayman who robbed travelers. He was known for cutting off fingers of his victims and stringing the fingers onto a garland that he wore around his neck. During the Buddha's travels, he came into the area frequented by Angulimala. The local villagers implored the Buddha to help them. On one of the Buddha's walks, he was spotted by Angulimala, who was perched on some boulders.

Angulimala yelled, "Stop" but the Buddha kept walking. Angulimala yelled, "You there, it is I, Angulimala who commands you to stop." The Buddha did not look up but just kept walking. Angulimala jumped down from the boulders, ran after the Buddha and confronted him, "What is the matter with you? Why don't you stop?" The Buddha looked directly into Angulimala's eyes and then quietly said, "I have stopped long ago. It is you who have not stopped."

Angulimala was shocked by both the Buddha's words and by his lack of fear. Angulimala undoubtedly was impressed by the Buddha, who had come not to punish but to help him. Perhaps Angulimala was "ready" to be rehabilitated and start a new life. Perhaps he simply did not know how to stop his criminal ways. Now, an option was opened to him. He prostrated himself before the Buddha and asked to become his disciple.

This story is an interesting historical account but it also can be used in one's own spiritual journey. Each of us can ask ourselves, "Why haven't I stopped?" Even if you don't know how you've become the kind of person you are, you can still stop doing things that hurt yourself and others. If you take the time to introspect, you can see many things you want to stop doing.

For example, say you want to stop martyring yourself when you feel unrecognized for working hard. Suppose people are coming over for a party and you feel put upon for having to get the house ready. You get stressed and snap at your spouse. Ironically, hard feelings result from the preparations for a happy occasion. How could this be handled differently?

I remember hearing about a couple, who were in the Peace Corps and were finishing their stay in a poor country. As a parting gift, a boy gave them a seashell. Knowing that the seashell could only be gotten from a distant beach, the couple thanked the boy for walking so far to get the seashell. The boy beamed and said, "Long walk part of gift." After that, whenever the couple felt they were martyring themselves by doing something from a sense of duty, one of them would remind the other of the joy of giving, by saying their personal code word, "Long walk."

We all can give back to the world in ways unique to our own circumstances. We can give back not out of a sense of "have to" but with a sense of joy. I know a teenager, who enjoyed helping stranded motorists. In winter he carried jumper cables in his car and he would stop to help motorists with dead batteries. He said proudly, "So far this winter, I've helped eight motorists; I want to go for double digits!"

When driving, most of us are in a hurry and feel we can't take the time to stop and help someone. Driving can be a metaphor for life. We are busy driving along and don't slow down or stop to think about what's really important in life. We don't stop to be grateful and give back for all that we have received.

There is a Japanese word *"On"* which commonly is translated as "obligation." We humans are said to have four kinds of *"On"* or obligations. The first obligation we have is to thank and repay what we have received from our parents. Next is our obligation to our family and friends, then to the society we live in, and finally to all living and non-living things in the world. We are interdependent and our lives as human beings are supported by all things. Of course, it is impossible to repay completely for all we have received. Our spiritual practice is to live with the attitude of wanting to try and repay an un-payable debt.

Typically, when we receive a gift or favor, we feel obligated to repay the kindness. Instead of fulfilling the obligation out of a sense of duty, we can open up to the joys of what I heard a minister call "the wonderful world of *On*." The first step is to stop taking things for granted. It is so easy for me to take things for granted that I need constant reminders to stop taking things for granted. Thus, I came to use the red stop signs and red light traffic signals as reminders to stop or pause mentally, and be aware of how I am living.

Part of my spiritual practice is to build up my "stopping power," which includes my wanting to stop my mindless receiving of things. I want to deepen my awareness of the causes and conditions that support my life. We all can benefit from building up "stopping power" which means to stop taking things for granted and to stop doing things that are harmful to ourselves, to others, and to the world we live in. Then we can start to give back. We can give back in many ways, not just by becoming involved in organized social causes. All of us can contribute by becoming more aware of the way we carry out our everyday activities.

For example, we can contribute to peace by stopping our aggressive driving or by stopping the negative way we talk to our spouses when we are impatient or irritated. Habits do not exist in a vacuum. It helps to stop and look at the factors that underlie and maintain our harmful habitual ways of behaving. We need to stop and examine our complacency and indifference. We need to stop ignoring how our lives influence and interact with other lives.

Developing "stopping power" reflects an attitude or commitment, whereby a person's life can be significantly changed. Such a change can occur suddenly through a traumatic event or crisis. The change can also occur and deepen gradually through sincere introspection and daily mindfulness.

I was impressed by an essay on braking titled "ABS" written by my brother Don. He wrote this essay regarding the Ashes Burial Service of our father. At the service, I chanted the Three Sacred Vows Sutra, and gave a minister's message or Dharma talk about making vows. In one part of my talk I said, "Everyone should make a sacred vow. What is the point of your life? What is the central thing your life rests on? There are many important things. It doesn't have to be one thing. Look deep within, see what the whole point of your life is, and make a commitment to it. Determine how you want to live your life and make your vow. Making a vow is an impressive thing but you have to make it happen. You can't just wait around. Standing here in a cemetery is certainly a place for us to become more aware of impermanence. We know we don't have all the time in the world. We have to be earnest, sincere and decide how we want to live our lives."

My brother Don wrote, "It occurred to me that the acronym for Ashes Burial Service is ABS.

This is also the acronym for the braking system on the automobile that prevents the wheels from locking up and causing an uncontrolled skid when you slam on the brakes in a panic stop. The ABS allows the wheels to continue turning so you can still steer the car to maintain control while bringing the car to a stop as quickly as possible."

He continues, "The subject of my brother's sermon was that we should all have our individual vow. My brother has the ability to personalize ideas and this 'vow' discussion was no exception. It really made me think about what my vow should be. At the same time, I thought that this ABS acronym should be applied; it will prevent any 'uncontrolled skids' while it brings me quickly to apply my vow without causing any crashes. In other words, it will allow me to apply my vow in a manner that will be clearly thought out and not be a 'flash in the pan.' What about my vow? I have several and I need to determine which one will be the best for me. I will use ABS to make the choice."

Whether as a metaphor or as an actual physical activity, driving can be a useful mindfulness tool. I try to use driving as part of my everyday spiritual practice. When approaching a traffic signal that's turning red, I put my foot on the brake pedal and push down. As I feel the pressure of my foot pushing down on the pedal, I say to myself, "Yes, slow down." I find that mindfulness is facilitated by having a bodily action accompany mental thought. Then, as I wait at the red light, I focus on my surroundings and become more aware of where I am. This helps me to "slow down" and focus on where I am spiritually, right now. Realistically, I don't do this kind of mindful stopping at every stop light, but maybe once or twice during a particular drive.

I like to think I am building up my general "stopping power" through the repetition of mindful stopping at the hundreds or even thousands of stop signs and stop lights over the years. I hope this "stopping power' will apply not only to my will-power regarding personal things, but also to stopping my apathy regarding involvement in important social issues. I'd like to think that when a social issue of concern occurs, I would have the courage of my convictions and be able to protest injustice by standing up and saying, "Stop." I want to feel I am doing my part to stop some of the suffering in the world.

Bright Dawn

SKY

Arriving at the lake, I park in front of Lee Street Beach. It is still half an hour before sunrise. In the quiet semi-darkness, a few runners glide by as gray shadows. I feel that the atmosphere is like an early morning service at a monastery. In fact, lakefront running is the equivalent of going to a religious service for me. The lakefront horizon is nature's altar. Before starting my run, I face the lake, and my eyes sweep across the entire horizon in awe. There can be no cathedral ceiling more magnificent than the vast sky above!

I think identifying with the sky is a universal human experience. Long ago it is what people who spent much of their time outdoors experienced when looking at the sky from the top of a mountain or across a wide prairie. Although such people perhaps were closer to nature than people today, all people experience peacefulness when in the big outdoors. There is a feeling that takes us out of ourselves and allows us to view our concerns from a wide perspective.

Having a wide perspective is called *"Takkan"* in Japanese. I came across this word in an essay written by my father. He explained how many unnecessary worries in life come from being attached to and victimized by a narrow, ego-centered view. *Takkan* means to take the long view of things; that is, to view the world with philosophic eyes.

Suffering often is relieved by putting the problem into a wider context than the immediate situation. However, due to strong feelings it is not always easy to take a wide view of things. It is hard to take a wide view when the difficulty involves conflicts with others. Whenever people are in conflict with one another, taking a wide view means to see the situation from the other person's perspective. A wide view means that other people count just as much as we do; that is, their needs are just as important as ours are. The conflict does not have to be expressed as, "My needs are more important than yours." The needs of both sides should be recognized as equally valid. Then it is easier to focus on resolving how the needs can be mutually met. Of course there are no guarantees, but resolution is more likely when things are seen from a wider perspective than just one's own position. Dualistic thinking such as, "I am right; you are wrong," only polarizes the problem and intensifies conflict. WAR can be an acronym for "We Are Right." Indeed, this describes what happens whether the "war" is a personal conflict between individuals or an armed confrontation between nations.

I like the saying, "Think Globally, Act Locally." The meaning of "Act Locally" is to live one's values here and now in our individual lives. It means to turn the abstract into something concrete. It is to walk on our talk. It means the path is always right before us, calling us to action.

"Think Globally" means to take a wide view beyond nationalistic, ethnic, and religious boundaries. Considering ourselves as citizens of the world is a basic priority that can harmonize with our other categories of belonging. We are all one as human beings. Our survival depends upon identifying with all living beings, and also with inanimate things. We must take care of ourselves, as well as the physical planet we live on.

Being able to take a wide view of things is the gateway to enlightened living. Spiritually, taking a wide view leads to wisdom, compassion, gratitude, reverence. A wide view ultimately becomes synonymous with all the virtues and precepts. Enlightened living means to live not only in harmony with others but with inner peace. We also need to take a wide view when the emotional conflict is within ourselves. Things often don't go the way we want, not because of others, but because that's the way life is. Looking at the sky can remind us to have a wide understanding of life's realities. Our minds and hearts can become as vast as the sky... big enough to take in all things. Instead, our usual narrow view is to see and cling to only "good" things. We do not want there to be any room for "bad" things in our lives. Such an unrealistic attitude causes many difficulties. When we embrace only the "good," we'll find there's a price to pay. If we deny the "bad," we'll miss out on valuable life lessons.

When struggling with the existential problem of life and death, we want to affirm life and deny death. Yet, the reality of life always includes death. They are like the two sides of one coin. When my son, Tate, was in college, one night he called home. His best friend's father had just died. This had a big impact on my son. He had to call and let us know he loved us. I felt for him. Could I help him in any way? Sooner or later, I was going to die and he would have to experience the sadness of losing a loved one. He would also have to deal with the reality of his own mortality.

How can one live in the midst of such existential anxiety yet stand above it? What is required is a wide view of life and death. Such a wide view goes beyond an intellectual perspective; it is a spiritual experience. For me, I relate taking a wide view with looking at the vast sky. The sky inspires me so much. Looking at the sky is a spiritual experience for me. I wrote my son a letter about this and gave it to him as a gift on his next birthday. I wrote:

Dear Tate,

This is a personal note from me to you. It's probably an overly sentimental, once-in-a-lifetime expression of my feelings. It is difficult for us to have an opportunity to talk about "heavy" stuff, namely death. It is not easy for two people, say father and son, to communicate and understand each other regarding ultimate concerns in life. Yet, if we can do that, all the rest of life's stuff is "gravy" because priority and perspective are firmly established.

To lose a loved one is *the* saddest thing in life. You know what I'm talking about because of what you experienced when you telephoned us after your best friend's father died. I want to offer you a teaching, a spiritual "tool," to use in dealing with *the* saddest thing . Without such teachings, it is easy to "sour" on life or get cynical and never have any sense of genuine contentment in life.

Each morning as I walk out to get the newspaper from the front lawn, I look at the sky from horizon to horizon. I take a deep breath and with a long exhale comes a gentle smile. Looking at the sky has turned into a daily spiritual practice for me. I feel embraced by the vast sky that surrounds and holds everything and everybody. I feel a unity or continuity with others. It makes me feel good to know that the sky is always there for our family. It's here for me in Illinois; it's there for others no matter where they are living. The sky is right there, any place and any time, just by looking up.

Look up and let that bigness, that vastness, widen your mind and heart. You see the sky in your own individual life but the sky also points to a universal truth. You can look up at the sky and know that you and I are one in the spiritual world of Oneness. The sky helps point us towards the Absolute, which is reality beyond all dualities... beyond life-death, win-lose, good-bad. When the truths of impermanence and interdependency are realized, a life of acceptance and appreciation opens up.

I look at the sky every day. Join me. Whenever you are mad or sad, look at the sky. Whenever you feel lonely, look at the sky. Whenever you get bogged down in self-centered concerns, look at the sky. The wide view of the sky can bring us together in good times, bad times, and all the in-between times. The sky is a symbol of Universal Life. Whenever you look at the sky you can be reminded that your individual life is one with Universal Life. This is true for me too, so to personalize it, whenever you look at the sky, you and I are one. We are one in Universal Life, which is the Absolute Reality that transcends space and time.

Being able to see and internalize the wide view of the sky is a watershed event in my own continuing spiritual journey. It means so much to me and I feel so fortunate and grateful. I offer the spiritual practice of looking at the sky as a precious gift to you. Unwrap and open this gift;

that is, bring it into your life. It does not matter if you ever become "religious" or not. It does not matter whether you become connected to an established set of beliefs and practices. It doesn't matter whether you become affiliated with a temple or congregation. Spirituality is another matter. Spirituality is private, personal, and goes beyond established forms. Of course, spirituality and traditional religion are not necessarily mutually exclusive. Although one can give rise to the other, the most important thing is your own inner spirituality.

Identifying with the wide view of the sky can help you cope with the inevitability of death. There are still tears as we struggle with all the things that make us human, but at the deepest level there is clarity and acceptance. In your spiritual journey, I offer you the simple daily practice of looking at the sky. I hope this, together with other experiences in your life, can give you a watershed event that you can pass on to your children and loved ones. I want this for you.

You should also know that the sky is a special symbol in Buddhism. Just as the sky is a vast emptiness, the sky in Buddhism refers to the Absolute Emptiness that goes beyond all conceptual dichotomies such as life-death or good-bad. It is *Absolute* Emptiness because it is not emptiness as opposed to fullness. It is beyond the duality of empty-full. Absolute Emptiness is not a static entity but is the dynamic flow of reality that can be called Universal Life.

The calligraphy character for sky is called "KU" in the Sino-Japanese pronunciation. In Buddhist sutras, there is constant reference to "KU." It symbolizes infinity and eternity, the formless and timeless truth of reality as it is. Since the calligraphy character for sky is pronounced "KU," you could look at the sky and say "KU" as your private "mantra." For personal impact, think of our Kubose family and say, "KU...bose." Tate, never lose your sense of humor!

Love, Dad

Bright Dawn

WATER

Before starting my lakefront run, I stand at the shore and look out at Lake Michigan. The view is almost the same as looking at an ocean. Lake Michigan is so large that the other shore is not visible; it's water as far as the eye can see. In fact, when my grandparents drove from California to visit us in Chicago, my grandfather saw Lake Michigan. He turned to his wife, and jokingly said, "Oh, I made a big mistake! I missed the turnoff for Chicago. Look, it's the Atlantic Ocean!"

The hugeness of an ocean is a teaching. In ancient sutras, the mind of the Buddha is often said to be a great ocean-mind. The Buddha's mind is large enough to receive and accept all things and purify them, just as the ocean receives all the dirty waters of rivers and purifies them all. Of course we have to be ecologically careful because even the ocean can become polluted. However, we can still apply the teaching that by having a great ocean-mind, we can take in all things and not be upset by them. We can also be flexible like water. Water changes its form according to the receptacle it is put in. When water is put into a round pail, it becomes round. Instead of being stubborn, we can be like water, and adapt ourselves according to the situation. It is said that wisdom is none other than flexibility of attitude.

There is something very peaceful about looking at a large body of water. A calmness arises from watching the constant motion of waves. The sounds of water and wind are natural and evoke a restful feeling of being in the midst of nature. When my father was in his 90's and staying at my place, I liked to take him to the lake. I would say to him, "I heard a rumor that Lake Michigan disappeared!" He'd say, "Yeah!?" I'd say,

"We'd better go check and see if it's still there." We'd go watch the waves come rolling in and just quietly sit together, not saying much.

My father passed away in March of 2000 at the age of 94. He lived a long, productive life of spreading the Dharma teachings. He was able to touch and influence many people in his over 60 years of ministry. We received many condolence letters. One Shin Buddhist minister wrote, "I am certain, as with the case of Shinran Shonin, your father, like the waves of Wakano Ura Bay, will return time and time again. Continuing, as long as the need is present, to expound the Dharma, in Oneness now with the Amida Tathagata. Serving, as he did in life, as a beacon of Light in a world that essentially dwells in darkness." I often think about these words when I see the waves on Lake Michigan roll rhythmically to the shore.

When I am asked, "Do Buddhists believe in an afterlife?" I often answer with a wave/ocean analogy. Individual human beings are like waves in the vast ocean. The ocean represents eternal, infinite truth. Truth is reality; the way things are. First let me describe the nature or reality of waves. Each wave is unique yet all waves consist of water. Each wave that rises up from the ocean, will also return to the ocean. A wave is not a piece of plastic or some static, unchanging object. A wave has its own particular shape but this shape is a constantly changing flow of water. Due to certain conditions such as the wind and water currents, a wave is "born." It lives its life flowing along the ocean surface. When a wave "dies," it does not go to a calm, heaven-like harbor where a lot of waves are bobbing around. When a wave "dies" it goes back to the ocean from where it originally came. Actually, to talk of coming and going is misleading because at no time is any wave ever separate from the ocean.

Nothing exists as a completely separate, unchanging entity. Everything exists as a dynamic constantly changing process. This also holds for human beings, and is the Buddhist teaching of *anatman* or selflessness. There is no "self" as an unchanging entity. To express this truth not from a narrow self-centered human perspective but from the wide perspective of absolute reality, is to say that there is no birth or death as such but rather only one eternal change. A finite human being is never separate from the infinite.

As I look at the shoreline of Lake Michigan, there are places where families have scattered ashes of their loved ones. The scattering of ashes into a lake or ocean is not uncommon. The reason given might be, "He loved to fish" or "This was his favorite spot." I think such acts also symbolize how the particular is always "one" with the universal. An individual life is one with Universal Life, just as a wave is one with the ocean.

Waves also can remind us of events in our lives, sometimes calm and sometimes stormy. Yet, viewing a wide expanse of water can give one a feeling of eternity. Whenever I come to the lake-front, no matter what the weather is like, even if the waves are rough and crashing on the shore, I feel a peace inside of me.

Bright Dawn

RUNNING

There is a joy in running that is somehow elemental or basic. I started running in the streets of my neighborhood but soon discovered the attractions of the lakefront path with trees and bushes in wide-open spaces, sea gulls flying gracefully over the lake, and the vast sky and water stretching to the horizon. Since Lake Michigan is to the east of Chicago, a sunrise over the lake can be spectacular. During the predawn period of about 15 minutes before the sun breaks the horizon, the clouds along the horizon turn beautiful shades of red. Whenever possible, I try to arrive during this predawn period.

I run in all kinds of weather. A nasty winter wind in the face is not nice but I remind myself that the same wind will be at my back later on. By running the same route during the different seasons, I am able to notice the changing faces of nature. Over the years I became more observant and began paying more attention to the details of my surroundings. After spring rains I noticed the different green shades of the moss growing on certain trees, and during autumn, the different patterns of how the leaves of particular trees turned color.

Just spending more time at the lakefront has enabled me to see different things— a squadron of geese flying in formation skimming over the waves, seagulls diving straight down into the water for fish, a crow going deep inside a trash can to get some leftover French fries. I also get a nice feeling seeing other regular runners. There was a woman with a long blond ponytail who ran with two Alaskan huskies on leashes that clipped onto a special harness around her waist. One man trained his two malamutes to pull by having them drag a large tire. A local minister I know would shout out humorous comments when we happened to pass one another. One time he yelled, "What is the sound of one leg running?"

I begin running north from Lee Street Beach. The sound of gravel crunching under my shoes is one of my favorite sounds, especially in the early morning stillness. I start running slowly and get into my own easy rhythm. I am the slowest runner at the lakefront. I have never passed another runner. Fast walkers have passed me by. I don't mind; I just smile and say to myself, "Just call me speedy rabbit!"

Sometimes I see another runner who is going really slowly, just barely shuffling along. Then I realize that he is going faster than I am. This makes me wonder how slow I must look. One time I came around a bend in the path and there was an older man walking his dog. When he saw me chugging along he smiled and said, "I guess you just have to keep on going."

"Keep going" became my personal mantra. I relate this to my spiritual journey too. There are no shortcuts or secret teachings. One just keeps going— that's it. Persistence and determination are just as important in life as being talented and having skills. Spiritually, we may value significant insights and experiences, but the most important thing is to keep going.

"Keep going" is not just an expression of reassurance and encouragement. "Keep going" also means not to rest on one's laurels, not to get caught in one's own conclusions, and not to think one has found final answers. In a spiritual journey, one never arrives; one is always traveling and learning. I think this "Keep Going" is a good basic teaching, similar to Shunryu Suzuki Roshi's famous "Beginner's Mind" or Korean Zen Master Sueng Sahn's "Don't Know Mind."

To keep "Don't Know Mind" means not to be victimized by one's discriminating mind; it means not to be caught by name or form. True "Don't Know Mind" is even beyond the dualistic labels of "knowing" and "not knowing." Whether the disciple says, "I know" or "I don't know," the Zen master gives him 30 blows! I like to loosen up Dharma students by telling them, "You're going to get lashed with a wet Dharma noodle!" Laughing together is one of life's greatest joys.

In the true "Beginner's Mind" there are no thoughts of attainment or non-attainment. As Suzuki Roshi says, "In the beginner's mind there is no thought of 'I have attained something.' All self-centered thoughts limit our vast mind. When we have no thought of achievement, no thought of self, we are true beginners. Then we can really learn something." He goes on to say that a beginner's mind is "an empty mind and a ready mind. If your mind is empty, it is always ready for anything; it is open to everything. In the beginner's mind there are many possibilities; in the expert's mind there are few."

"Keep going" means to be truly open-minded. Some of us may think we are open-minded and willing to listen to new ideas, but rarely are we really open-minded about life itself. We close our minds to undesired changes in life. We cling to our ideas about youth, health, and mortality. We have trouble accepting the realities of old age, illness, and death.

In Buddhism, we don't talk about sin but consider ignorance as the basic human condition. Actually our ignorance is not due to a lack of knowledge but rather due to our ignoring of the basic truths in life. Thus, it has been said that we do not suffer from ignorance but from "ignore-ance." We ignore the fact that life is a very dynamic, changing process. We close our ego-centered minds to life's fundamental realities.

"Keep going" means to take a wide view of life. Like the vast open sky that keeps going from horizon to horizon, we can take in all things, wanted and unwanted. "Keep going" means to alter our usual attitude or approach to life. We have to change our understanding of the nature of purpose and meaning in life. We might ask ourselves, "Well, if we take the wide view of always 'keep going,' how can we accomplish anything? Shouldn't we have goals in life?" Being goal-oriented is okay in that it provides a direction or an impetus for our actions. Yet, an important teaching in life is, "The means equals the end." That is, the real joy is in the doing itself. A similar saying is, "Don't concentrate on the pursuit of happiness; instead, concentrate on the happiness of pursuit."

Separate the journey from the destination. Life is not a problem to be solved. It is okay to "live the question." We don't have to have the final answer to everything. "Keep going" means we do not have to victimize ourselves by always judging good or bad about what is happening. "Keep going" means not being trapped by name or form. "Keep going" means not being caught by praise or blame. Joy or sorrow, keep going. Success or failure, keep going. No need for a superiority or inferiority complex, keep going. This is the spiritual life of liberation and enlightenment. This is how to live an absolute life in a relative world. Be yourself, freely walking in the world, just as you are.

When I am running, I let myself be one with running. If I feel tired or unmotivated, I just keep going. If I feel great, I don't get caught up in that either; I just keep going. This morning as I leave the Lee Street Beach area, I "keep going" and continue along the lake towards a children's playground about 200 yards ahead. The path is only about 15 feet from the lake. Randomly stacked boulders, about five feet high, separate the path from the lake. About 50 yards before the playground, there's a large tree to the right of the path. Just after this tree is a metal park regulations sign. A few feet beyond this sign is a rectangular boulder with a level surface, in contrast to the surrounding unevenly surfaced boulders.

This flat boulder always caught my attention as I ran by it. It seemed to invite me to stop and stand on it. So I began doing that, pausing to look at the horizon over the lake. Sometimes I would stand on this boulder and throw my arms out wide to take in the vast sky. Other times I would kneel down on top of it and enjoy a quiet moment of reflection. Being on this flat boulder invokes in me a sense of calm power, reassuring

Power Spot

me everything is okay and encouraging me to keep going forward strongly— both in the day's run and also in my life. I call this flat boulder my "power spot" because it is a place where I have empowered and motivated myself in many ways.

An amazing coincidence happened at the location of my power spot. A large turtle, four feet in diameter, carved out of pink rock, was propped halfway up on my power boulder. Some local artist must have donated his work to the public lakefront. It amazed me that this turtle symbolizing persistence and a spirit of "keep going" had been placed on my power boulder. The turtle's head was stretched upward with his mouth wide open in a shout to the sky. I often patted the turtle's head as I ran by.

One day, after a month or so, I was shocked to see that the turtle had been broken into pieces. The rock turtle being destroyed may seem like a sad incident but I will always carry the image of that rock turtle within me. I am reminded of a teaching called "Tokusan's Candle."

Tokusan was an earnest student of Buddhism. In his travels, he stopped to meet with Ryutan, a Buddhist teacher. Tokusan was amazed that there was so much to be learned that was not in books. The discussion lasted late into the night. It was pitch dark when Tokusan started to leave. Tokusan lit a candle and was about to step outside when Ryutan blew the candle out! At that moment Tokusan's mind was opened; he understood.

In this story, what did Tokusan understand? He was very learned about the Buddhist teachings; he knew all the terminology and concepts. He possessed them as though they were his, but they were external things. They were not his; instead, he belonged to them. If one's peace or happiness depends upon external things, then that kind of peace or happiness is fragile. Most of us are too dependent on external things such as wealth, fame, and even sacred scriptures. Then when life hits us hard, we find nothing helps us.

One has to find out in one's own life what Tokusan found. Tokusan was depending upon a candle to guide him through the darkness. However, Ryutan blew out the candle. In one's life, one cannot wholly depend upon external "candles." Yes, candles give off light but a wind might blow them out. Then, what is to be done? Buddhism points to that which cannot be extinguished. One must have peace from within, from the center of one's life. One can discover the true life that has an internal light, which can never be blown out.

Buddhism teaches freedom and this comes about when one is not dependent upon external things. Thus, we cannot rely on an external God, Buddha, or a rock turtle to truly empower us. We can respect them but should not rely on them. Such external things can point to the way but are not the way themselves. Concepts are our own mental constructions; in certain contexts useful, but in reality their existence depends upon how we interact with them.

Spiritually, there is only the oneness of an individual life flowing within the dynamic reality of Life itself. We can give conceptual labels to this dynamic reality, but it is a mistake if we allow such external concepts to become more real than the very reality to which they point. I think of this teaching when I go by the place where the pink rock turtle used to be. Chunks of pink rock can still be seen scattered among the boulders.

Once I climbed over the boulders and to my surprise saw a baby rock turtle. This turtle, about

Rock Turtle

18 inches in diameter, cannot be seen from the path because it is on the lake side of the boulders. Whenever I go by this area I smile, knowing there is a hidden baby turtle that escaped destruction.

When I decided to take a picture of the baby rock turtle, I had to climb over the boulders. Not being as agile as when I was younger, I slipped and bruised my knee. About a week later, the wound's scab came off and I looked at my knee. I saw an oval-shaped scar and exclaimed, "It looks just like a turtle's back!" I thought, "Now I have a reminder of that baby rock turtle for the rest of my life!" Human projection is an interesting phenomenon without it having to be linked to superstitious thinking.

As I continue running along the path, the children's playground is just ahead. Where the path begins to curve around the playground, two small trees arch over the gravel path. As I pass under this arch, I think of flower arches used at weddings. Weddings remind me how important relationships are in life. A wedding represents the highest promise of an idealistic relationship.

Thinking of weddings, I remember seeing a marriage proposal while running at the lakefront. One part of my running route is paved. One day I came upon some words that were chalked on the asphalt path. There was one word every 6 or 7 feet. As I walked along, I read the message.

"There ... is ... a ... moment ... in ... life ... when ... you ... miss ... someone ... so ... much ... that ... you ... want ... to ... pick ... them ... up ... from ... your ... dreams ... and ... hug ... them."

Then there was a series of arrows that led to the sentence, "Will you marry me?" I had to smile as I wondered if this was a real question. Had a young man taken his girlfriend for a walk along this path? If so, I hope she said, "Yes" and I wish them well. Realistically, even with the sincerest of vows, any couple will have problems. Our relationships provide a real richness in life but they also can bring great emotional pain.

We humans are social animals. There can be misunderstandings and difficulties in any relationship, whether between husband and wife, between friends, or among co-workers. Why is it that we get frustrated and upset? How do we handle problems in a relationship? Typically we blame the other person. We think that things would be okay if the other person changed and were to act in a different way. We have strong feelings like, "I am right; you are wrong." "I'm doing my share but you're not doing your share."

In most relationships, the typical attitude is that each person should give 50%. The thinking is that $50\% + 50\% = 100\%$. However, love's arithmetic is $100\% + 100\% = 100\%$. This is Life's arithmetic too. Each person can live his or her life 100% with no regret. To love and live 100% means to respect one's individual uniqueness and the absolute value of one's life. It is only when one truly respects oneself that the uniqueness and absolute value of others are also respected.

When two people respect one another, each person takes responsibility for his or her own well-being. They do not make the mistake of thinking that one's happiness is dependent upon the other.

Wedding Arch

The arch I run under is formed by two trees, each *independently* rooted, which lean and come together. Although I call this arch a wedding arch, it can symbolize the importance of all loving relationships. As I run under the arch, I wish the best for all people, including myself, in all our relationships. May we be free from the tyranny of our expectations of others. May we love unconditionally and may we not take any of our relationships for granted.

Relationships can be fragile, like the two trees gently intertwined over the path. Seeing the delicate togetherness of the arch reminds me that relationships need patient, kind nurturing. One of the Buddha's teachings is the Eightfold Path: Right Understanding, Thoughts, Speech, Action, Livelihood, Effort, Mindfulness, and Meditation.

Right Speech is especially important in our relationships because much of our interpersonal interaction is talking to one another. Right Speech means to speak in a sincere and kind manner. It means not using "honesty" as an excuse to engage in judgmental blaming and malicious criticism. If one cannot say something constructive, one should keep a "noble silence." Do not speak carelessly. Treat your mouth as if it were a loaded gun. Remember that words are powerful.

My wife and I raised two boys, who were two years apart in age. When the boys were growing up, I devised a family code word "NS" which stood for "Negative Speech." Negative speech was whenever one of our sons said something to make the other one feel bad. For example, "I have more pop to drink than you do" or "I'm better at this than you are." Whenever one of our sons felt hurt by such a comment, he would say, "NS." This was simply to give immediate feedback to the offender of his inappropriate comment. Although there was no added parental lecturing or consequences imposed, the use of "NS" alone dramatically reduced the occurrence of negative speech between our two sons.

My sons also observed that I often used a gruff voice in family interactions. They used the code term "MT" for "Mean Talk" whenever they felt I talked to them in a "mean" voice. I welcomed such feedback and it made me more aware of how I was speaking. However, even today when I honestly assess how I speak to family members, I still am struggling with my "MT" problem.

Despite good intentions and insights, difficulties will occur in all relationships. When we hurt another person's feelings, we can learn from the experience and try to handle similar situations in a better way next time. When we are the one who is hurt by someone, we can try to understand the reason for the other person's actions and try not to harbor any festering resentment. This is easier said than done. Yet, it is situations that involve emotions like resentment that can benefit the most from being able to take a wide view. In most families, there are many daily opportunities to practice taking a wide view of things. Many of us are such slow learners! Too often we take a wide view only when pushed to do so— and then we feel even more resentment! Instead, consider the taking of a wide view as a daily discipline, as a spiritual practice. Be motivated by a sincere wish or vow to take a wide view of all situations.

As individuals, we can decide what kind of person we want to be and what kind of life we want to live. This can be an unconditional and unilateral decision that is not dependent on how others act. Holding grudges and not being able to let go of resentments is a major reason for discontent in life. Misunderstanding with a friend? Harsh words from a loved one? The secret to happiness is sometimes said to be a poor memory. Here, wide view means to clean yesterday off your eyeglasses and see today as a completely new day. Young children and our animal pets forget yesterday's frustrations and greet each day with fresh enthusiasm. In their natural innocence, they know how to keep going.

In our interpersonal interactions, some things are worth remembering while other things are best forgotten. Wisdom is knowing the difference. In a sense, wisdom is having a selective poor memory. In one of the Buddhist sutras it is said:

> *Some people are like letters carved in rock; they are easily angered and they keep their angry thoughts for a long time. Some people are like letters written in sand; they give way to anger also, but the angry thoughts quickly pass away. Some people are like letters written on water; they let verbal abuse pass them by and no disturbing thoughts are retained.*

Idealistic goals are often unrealistic when they are viewed only as goals to be reached. I prefer to see idealistic goals as simply pointing out a direction I want to head in. I continue running on the path. After the "Wedding Arch," I pass the children's playground, go by tennis courts and Dempster Beach, where kayaks and windsurfing boards can be put into the lake. Just beyond a restroom building is a tall Ginkgo tree. I like the distinctive fan-shaped leaves of this ancient

Ginkgo

tree species from China. From another time and place this species through countless unbroken seedling-tree generations is here right now.

In the same way, Buddhist teachings from over 2500 years ago in India are alive and well here in America. All religious traditions represent the compassion of past teachers for the benefit of future generations. Trees stand tall and have a long life span. They provide shade for travelers. Seeing the ancient species of Ginkgo tree evokes in me feelings of respect and gratitude for being able to take spiritual shelter under the broad branches of the religious traditions that have been passed on for countless generations.

As I run past the Ginkgo tree, I nod my head in a slight bow and continue on the path. About 75 yards ahead in an open clearing on the left side, there are picnic tables. Behind this picnic area is a tree shaped like an upside-down heart. The tree's outline is ragged and thin, without much foliage. It seems like such a delicate tree to me, especially compared to the thickly-leafed trees surrounding it. This "Heart Tree" gives me a teaching about having heart or courage. Not the kind of courage needed to face physical danger but a resilient, steady courage that's needed when you're knocked upside down and the edges of your

Heart Tree

life are ragged and thin. Life breaks us all but we heal and are stronger at the broken places.

It takes courage to live and love unconditionally. It takes courage to be vulnerable. Although it takes courage to deal with problems in life, it takes even more courage to acknowledge that often the problem is oneself and not outside conditions or other people. Do you want to excuse the way you are now by blaming what happened to you in the past? Get over it! Realize that "X" is not the problem but that how you deal with "X" is the problem. "X" can be anything; such as a bad domestic situation, financial troubles, or health problems.

A trivial example comes to mind but the example still can make the point of moving from an external or other-perspective to an internal or self-perspective. When taking my morning shower, I noticed the cap was left off the shampoo bottle... again! I've told my wife countless times this was messy and also allowed the shampoo to evaporate. This is a little thing but I take it personally. She doesn't listen to me; she doesn't respect me. I feel I've been wasting my time and energy trying to straighten her out. Whoaa... "X," the shampoo cap being left off, is not the problem. How I deal with "X" is the problem. The ways I've been using have led to frustration and getting upset because I was seeing the situation as my wife's problem, not mine. Well then, how can I deal with *my* problem? I can realize the situation is not really an economic matter of wasting or losing shampoo through evaporation. Is having an argument over a three-dollar bottle of shampoo worth it? Expressed like that, as a comparison of three dollars versus the quality of our relationship— it's a non-issue.

As to the cap being left off as messy, am I a neat freak? What's the big deal? Loosen up! By looking at the situation in a different way, I can deal with my problem. Ironically, because of the way I began handling the situation, my wife began to get better at remembering to replace the cap. We both became more considerate of each other. This is a simple example. Other problems in life are more complex and involve deeper emotions, but the same psychological process is involved in shifting from "X" is the problem to realizing that how one deals with "X" is the real problem.

It should be mentioned that when one can easily change external aspects in dealing with a situation, there is no problem. The situations that are problems are those in which one has little control or power to change the situation. That is, such situations involve the kind of problems that require changing oneself. For example, the problem is not that people are slow and stupid. The problem is that one is stressed and impatient. If one doesn't realize that the problem is with oneself, the problem will never be dealt with successfully. If one doesn't change oneself, one will *always* feel one has to deal with "slow and stupid" people.

What happens when your ego blames external factors as the cause of your misery? You get frustrated and angry or get depressed and perhaps give up completely. Anger leads to "acting out" behavior that does not help the situation, and only makes things worse. Anger is like burning one's house down to get rid of a rat. Giving up and feeling sorry for yourself is a dangerous swampy place. Watch your footing. Don't get caught in the quicksand of cynicism. Don't drown in your own martyrdom.

It is hard to see that oneself is the root cause of one's problems and then even harder to do something about it. To do this takes not only some understanding and insight but also some "heart" and courage. Go beyond judgmental blaming of others or yourself; focus on constructive action. It is easy to get mad or sad. Let go of a narrow egocentric view and open up to a broader view of yourself in the world. Rather than just cursing or lamenting the darkness, light a candle.

Going beyond ego-centered emotions can be a life-changing lesson in living life and dealing with the world. It is the gateway to wisdom and compassion. Buddhism is the way of Absolute Subjectivity, which is self-responsibility through a total, unilateral empowerment. An existential courage is needed to handle life itself. This kind of courage means to keep going regardless of what life brings. As expressed by Maya Angelou, "Life loves to be taken by the lapel and told, 'I'm with you, kid. Let's go!' "

The Buddhist response to tragedy and suffering, whether one's own or in the world, is to cultivate wisdom. As we learn to deal with suffering wisely, we have empathy with others who are also suffering. Introspective courage applied to one-self leads to compassion for others. As I run by the "Heart Tree," it reminds me to have courage and compassion. To have "heart" means to be strong and keep going, and it also means to help others. All of us can benefit from receiving and giving some courage and compassion.

KEEP GOING

The "Wedding Arch" and the "Heart Tree" are teachings when viewed through spiritual eyes. More trees ahead offer me glimpses of certain spiritual qualities. I approach a pond built with a perimeter of limestone bricks. On a small island in the pond is a majestic willow tree. This tree has a noble, serene quality, even when the wind is blowing through its branches. It is said that the wise are not shaken by the winds of praise or blame. It is a wise person, indeed, who does not allow others to define his or her goodness or badness. Seeing the willow tree gives me a deep feeling of majestic nobility that is every individual's birthright.

Just prior to publishing this book, a fierce wind storm blew down the willow tree. I wondered what I could write about this. Is it a lesson in humility since not even the most magnificent and most noble are exempt from the winds of change? I guess the point is, we are always judging or evaluating what happens. Do we always have to decide that something is either good or bad?

Willow Tree

I am reminded of a story about a man who bought a horse for his young son. The horse was a birthday gift and the father was so pleased to be able to do this for his son. However, shortly afterwards, the son had a riding accident. He fell off the horse and broke his leg. The father lamented, "Oh, I shouldn't have bought that horse." A few years went by and because of a war, young men were being drafted into the army. However, the son was not drafted because of his past broken leg. The father was glad that his son didn't have to go to war and possibly be killed.

This story illustrates that as conditions and circumstances change, so do our judgments of whether a given event is considered good or bad. As ancient Greek philosophers have stated, "Nothing is good or bad, only our thinking makes it so." We humans consider death a bad thing and something to be avoided. Yet, in the scheme of nature, both life and death are natural occurrences and are beyond any labels of good or bad. Although as humans we cannot help but mourn the death of our loved ones, our sadness can be tempered with the wisdom of taking a wider view of things.

In the case of the fallen willow tree, the park district quickly replaced it with a young willow tree. We might think, "Well, out with the old and in with the new; life goes on." As I thought about this willow tree situation, it does demonstrate the reality of impermanence and constant change. At the same time there is the reality of interdependency. On the physical level, the new tree will benefit from the compost of the old tree that has been left behind in the soil. As the new tree grows, the old tree will be a part of it.

These were some of my thoughts as I pondered the demise of the willow tree. It was difficult to take a wide view of things when I was staring at the fallen tree right in front of me. Then I began to sense that the deficiency was in me for not being able to see that the willow still retained its quiet dignity even in its broken state. I thought about how this was similar to when our loved ones age and we have to take care of them. As caretakers of elderly parents it is a challenge to accord them the dignity and respect they deserve when we have to deal with their physical limitations on a daily basis. Being patient and understanding is easier when we take a wide view of things. A view that is wider than just how we feel about things. The problem is not their aged or broken state but how we deal with the situation.

In any case, I was saddened by what happened to the willow tree, yet was able to understand and accept the natural path of life and death.

West of the willow tree is a small tree that is not readily noticed. This tree is more towards the street than the path. I happened to notice the tree when I took a detour off the path and ran on the grass. I call this tree the "Zen Tree" because there is a circle on the bark of the trunk about a foot off the ground.

One part of me just accepts that the circle is there on the tree. Another part of me wonders how did the circle get there. This wondering part of me notices that some of the trees in the park have a white area at the bottom of their trunks. Maybe this is due to the fact that mulch is piled high around the tree during the winter season. It also might be due to some chemical that is sprayed at the bottom of the trunks to prevent insect damage. Either of these possibilities would explain the white areas at the bottom of the trees but it doesn't explain the circle. I have to revert back to accepting that the circle is just there. However, I can explain why the circle leads me to call the tree a Zen Tree.

Circles have a long history in Zen Buddhism, particularly in painting and calligraphy. The circle, called *enso* in Japanese, has many

Zen Tree

meanings in Zen art. The circle is said to express both the emptiness and completeness of Absolute Reality or what is called *sunyata* in Sanskrit. The circle is seen as the all, the void, and enlightenment itself.

Circles have been used as teaching devices by Zen masters. Circles have been drawn in the sand with sticks. Circles have been drawn in the air with index fingers. My discovery of the Zen Tree is a good teaching provided by Mother Nature. Circles can remind us of such things as the cycle of the seasons and the orbits of the planets. Einstein said that space is curved. This means that if we went far enough in one direction, we would end up where we started from. I think this is nature's largest circle.

It has been said that Buddhist thinking or philosophy is like a circle rather than linear. Linear thinking is like a straight line, which has a beginning and an end. Linear thinking is dualistic because the beginning and the end are seen as two separate things. In this conception, goals are achieved by starting at the beginning of the line, and going forward to reach the goal at the end of the line. If we stop halfway, we did not succeed.

Buddhist thinking is non-dualistic; reality is not dichotomized into two opposites. When considering a circle, any point can be both a beginning and an end. This means that regardless of where one is at, one can begin a journey. It also means that one can find fulfillment at any point on the circle. Fulfillment (e.g. nirvana, enlightenment, the Pure Land) is possible right here, right now, in the "Pure Moment."

The present moment is both the starting and ending point. What a dynamic way of living! The end goal or fulfillment is simultaneously the beginning of the next adventure, and vice versa. Both life and nature are in constant change and movement. To live in accordance with such a dynamic reality means one always "keeps going." Rather than this "keep going" meaning one never reaches an end goal, it means one is always beginning/finishing or finishing/beginning.

Having thought and said all this about circles, I feel it is just "too much." This is why just seeing or drawing a circle is a more satisfying experience. The simplicity of the circle has a mystery about it that is beyond words. Yet, the circle conveys a lively sense of movement and an eternal timelessness. The circle is such a good expression of spirituality. I can only nod, smile, and put my hands together in Gassho when I see the circle on the "Zen Tree."

I continue running past the pond and a concession/restroom building. Just beyond a parking lot is a pair of small trees that look like they're doing a graceful dance together. I call them the "Jitterbugging Trees." Life is a dance! Some people take their religion too seriously in a reserved, pious way. This is why I prefer the word spiritual rather than religious. I don't mean spiritual as in spirits floating around but as in having a lively spirit. Spirituality means to have a passion for life, not just some kind of empty emotionalism. Spirited people have an enthusiastic energy that is contagious. Spirituality involves guiding such energy rather than muting it.

Life is filled with unexpected obstacles and difficulties that challenge us to meet them with a fullness of spirit. This is what the Buddha did when he encountered life's basic suffering. He did not seek escapist distractions nor did he remain emotionally detached. He shared his insights of the Dharma, the truth of life's reality.

Jitterbugging Trees

The teaching contained in his first discourse is called the Four Noble Truths: (1) Truth of suffering; (2) Truth regarding the cause of suffering; (3) Truth regarding the overcoming of suffering; (4) Truth regarding the living of an enlightened life. The Buddha looked at life with clear eyes and a warm heart. The world needs spiritual people who are inspired to live life with such noble qualities as wisdom and compassion.

What is wisdom and compassion? Consider again the saying, "Think Globally; Act Locally." Wisdom is to "Think Globally" and compassion is to "Act Locally." Wisdom is to never stop taking a wide view of things. We may start with individual concerns but our vision can widen to include the whole world.

In his poem, "Call Me By My True Name," Thich Nhat Hahn says that our understanding and empathy can be wide enough to include both the aggressor and the victim. Our compassion is for both the 12-year old refugee-boat girl raped by a sea pirate and also for the sea pirate whose heart is not yet capable of seeing and loving. Taking this kind of wide view is indeed a challenge for most of us.

Compassion is not just a noun or a feeling, but is a verb and a call to action. Compassion means to continually act and "keep going" in one's efforts. "Keep going" is a spirited shout:

The deluding passions are inexhaustible.
I vow to transcend them all.

The gates of Dharma are numberless.
I vow to open them all.

Sentient beings are countless.
I vow to help them all.

When we wholeheartedly vow to attain the unattainable, we just have to sing and dance with a lively spirit. The only true power in the world is the joy of unbridled compassion.

I am energized when I see the Jitterbugging Trees. With a smile, I continue running. Just ahead the path turns right, into Northwestern University property. Just past a sailing club building, the path makes a 90-degree turn to the north, and I make a surprising discovery.

As I slow down to make the turn, I happen to notice some faint writing spray painted on the paved path. I pause to look at the writing. Imagine my surprise to read the words, "keep going." This is a significant phrase for me since I had adopted it as a personal teaching some years ago. The faded script on the path is probably

Keep Going

left over from some marathon. I don't know
how old the writing is and I wonder why I never
noticed it before. I am always amazed at how
many "coincidences" seem to pop up whenever
I look around carefully.

BRIDGE TO INSPIRATION POINT

The path continues northward towards a large lagoon. A small bridge goes eastward towards the lake. Under this bridge, a school of large carp can sometimes be seen swimming. Chimney swifts are often flying from perches under the bridge to small nesting holes in the sand banks of the lagoon outlet that goes out to the lake.

Seeing the bridge, I start humming of one of my favorite songs, "Bridge Over Troubled Water." At first I feel the bridge represents the Dharma, and then that it's the Dharma itself that is singing out the lyrics, offering reassurance whenever we're troubled and feeling down. No doubt about it, the Dharma is a most excellent bridge to help us over difficult times. The Dharma refers to the law of cosmic order of existence in the universe. We cannot go wrong relying on the Dharma. The Dharma can never fail us because the Dharma is Absolute Truth, which is Reality-As-It-Is (not reality as we want it to be).

Bridge

On our spiritual journey, a bridge helps us travel from the shore of ignorance to the shore of wisdom. A bridge is a concrete way to express the movement of crossing over. When one crosses over, one is on a different piece of land. Any significant experience can function as a bridge whereby one can "cross over" and become a different person and live a new life.

In the movie "Thelma and Louise," one of the women has experiences that liberate her from a suffocating life with an insensitive husband. She knows she will not go back to being the way she was— she is changed. The woman tells her friend, "I've crossed over."

I try not to take any bridge for granted. I try to cross over in a mindful way. Just beyond the bridge I'm running on is a promontory I call Inspiration Point. The bridge that leads towards Inspiration Point is a small but sturdy bridge. I have an intimate, safe feeling while running on it. The bridge symbolizes my renewed intent to "cross over" and live an inspired life.

In a flash of insight I realize what the real bridge is for my spiritual journey: "I am the bridge." I am the one who has to be mindful and aware. I am the one who can make connections between the Dharma teachings and my everyday life. In this way I discover the enlightened world is here, now, in my ordinary world. The worlds are not two, but one. The Buddha said, "Be a lamp unto yourself." My equivalent is, "Be a bridge unto yourself."

After crossing the bridge, I follow the paved path to the right. There's a stone bench engraved "In Memory of Mimi." I look southward across the water to admire the Chicago skyline. As Chicagoans know, the "big three" downtown skyscrapers are the Sears Tower, the Hancock, and the Aon (formerly Standard Oil) building. I extend this notion of the "big three" to a religious context. Christians know their "big three" as the Trinity of the Father, Son, and Holy Spirit. In Buddhism there are many teachings related to the number three. One that has some similarity to the Christian Trinity is called Trikaya.

The Trikaya describes the three meanings or aspects of Buddhahood. My interpretation of the three aspects is as follows: The first is the Absolute (Dharmakaya in Sanskrit). This refers to the ultimate source of enlightenment; it is formless and timeless. The second is the Manifested (Nirmanakaya). This refers to Buddhahood that appears in our phenomenal world; such as, the historical Gautama Buddha. The third is the

Mimi's Bench

Spiritual (Sambhogakaya). This refers to the action or activity of enlightenment; that is, the spiritual qualities of wisdom and compassion.

Sometimes when I look out from Mimi's Bench, I make associations of the view with these three aspects of Buddhahood. I see the empty, infinite sky as symbolizing the Absolute aspect. Secondly, I consider the landscape of water and clouds, together with the skyline and all other things in the environment, as the Manifested aspect.

This means that all people and things in the world are my teachers. Thirdly, the Spiritual aspect is my joy and gratitude for being enabled to receive and experience the working of the absolute in this relative world.

Another reason the number three is important in Buddhism is because all Buddhists, regardless of denomination, value the Three Treasures or Triple Jewels of Buddhism, which are:

Buddha (enlightened teachers)

Dharma (the teachings)

Sangha (community of truth seekers)

It should be clarified that although teachers and the teachings are worthy of great respect and gratitude, they are not deified as objects to be worshipped in and of themselves. In Buddhism it is said that teachers and teachings are like a finger pointing to the moon (enlightenment), and that one should not mistake the finger for the moon. Do not get fixated on the finger; look beyond to what the finger is pointing at.

In commenting on the Three Treasures, I like to think of the Sangha as not only my fellow Buddhists but as including all living things; all are seeking to live their own true lives, and all are worthy of respect.

The word Dharma has different nuances in meaning. The Dharma was not created or invented by the Buddha. The Dharma is not a set of beliefs to be believed in but is the truth of life, reality As-It-Is. The Buddha realized and lived the Dharma. For over forty years after his enlightenment, he shared his experiences with others. His expression of the Dharma can be summarized into three basic teachings:

> Impermanence / constant change
> The Buddhist view of the world

> Interdependency / non-self
> The Buddhist view of life

> Enlightenment / Nirvana
> The Buddhist view of truth

The Buddha is not a savior who is prayed to for salvation. There is no petitionary prayer in Buddhism. Buddhists practice meditation, which is to be mindfully in the moment. Prayer is talking; meditation is listening. Of course, in a broader sense, prayer can mean to quietly commune or be one with the absolute.

With regard to the word Buddha, it is important to emphasize that the Buddha is not a deity. In Buddhism the concept of God is neither affirmed nor denied. The assertions regarding theism, atheism and even agnosticism are all based on the dualism of God or no God. The Buddhist approach, however, is non-dualistic. That is, truth or reality is beyond yes vs. no or being vs. non-being. This is why in Buddhism the ultimate cause or essential nature of things is called Absolute Emptiness or "Suchness."

Differences in terminology are often a problem in a religiously pluralistic society. Non-dualistic Buddhist expressions can be difficult to understand. One has to be careful not to misunderstand or jump to a wrong conclusion. This is why Buddhists use words like ignorance rather than sin; and enlightenment, rather than salvation. Yet, no matter what words are used, universal spiritual truths are great but the religious tongue is so short.

Whenever I run by Mimi's Bench, I glance at the architectural "big three" of the famous Chicago skyline. Then I think of how the number three is used in Buddhism. Fortunately, my thoughts are always brief because only a few yards ahead, Inspiration Point draws my attention. Despite the boulders that have been garishly painted by university students, there is a feeling of nature's wildness as waves crash against the boulders on this promontory point.

As I stand and look out at the lake, I feel that everything I've experienced during the morning run is with me. The experiences have become a part of me like digested food, providing fuel and energy to live an inspired life. I breathe deeply as though I want to take in even more inspiration from the wide expanse of water and sky. I spread out my arms and yell, "Yes!"

When standing at Inspiration Point, sometimes I shout a phrase out over the water. I've come to call such phrases, "Shouting Words." "Shouting Words" express what I am feeling at the time. Many of my "Shouting Words" are idiosyncratic, like personal code words. Other people would not understand their full meaning without knowing the context or story behind such words.

Shouting has become a spiritual practice for me. I've shouted in a closet at home, in my car, on mountain tops, next to a rushing water fall, and when a loud train whizzes by. Some "Shouting Words" can deepen their impact over time and become "Turning Words." "Turning Words" are words that can turn one's life around. They are like mantras that summarize and empower one's personal philosophy of life. When my niece and her friend were visiting from California, I took them to see the sunrise at Inspiration Point. While we were there, I described and did my shouting practice. Then, they did their own shouting too. My niece shouted, "Live life 100% with no regret!" Her friend shouted, "Be true to yourself!"

Shouting reminds me of a passage written by my father's teacher, Rev. Haya Akegarasu,

> "There are two languages: one's own language and a language for the other. The first is the shout and the second is propaganda. Of course one's tears and blood may be found in propaganda. But it is still very different from the shout, which is entirely one's own language. Those who have no life of their own are always making combinations out of other people's words. No matter what such people say, they are not moved by it, so they cannot move others. If someone is 'moved' it is only by a mechanical agreement to be moved. I want to hear words that are like sparks from red-hot iron pounded by a hammer, or like drops of blood, or like a stream of tears..."

Although using "Shouting Words" as a spiritual practice is not the same as a spontaneous shout, one does feel something beyond ordinary verbal expressions. A solitary shout to the open sky gives me a feeling of nakedly exposing my inner self to the whole universe. Then I feel the universe reassuring and encouraging me, "Okay, I'm with you. Now, let's go do something."

As I stand at Inspiration Point, I see a bright spot glowing on the horizon. The reflection of light off the clouds is so bright that one cannot help but feel something of great power is just below the horizon. It is apparent the sunrise is coming soon.

Bright Dawn

BRIGHT DAWN

It is always a dramatic moment when the tip of the sun breaks the horizon. "There it is!" The spark of bright light flashes across the sky, penetrating my eyes and flooding my insides with warmth. I watch, struck silent with wonder, as the sun rises quite rapidly and becomes completely visible in only a few minutes. The sun is a luminous red disk when it is just above the horizon. As the sun rises higher, it becomes bright yellow and one cannot look directly at it anymore. Just before I cannot look directly at it anymore, I stare intently at the sun's brightness and fix the moment in my mind. On later occasions whenever lighting a candle at home, I would stare intently at the bright center of the candle flame and be reminded of the sun's brightness. In this way, whenever I took the time to mindfully look upon any object, the object would glow with a life of its own— yet this life also would resonate with my own— and I would feel a kinship that transcended the usual subject-object split. At such times, my hands come together palm-to-palm in oneness. In the same way, I put my hands together and bow to the sun when I see the sunrise. The suchness (naturalness) of nature provides simple but deep teachings. The spirituality lies not in worshipping nature but in the experience of being one with nature.

On this particular morning I have brought with me three small pebbles from my backyard. I make a "pebble offering" by tossing the pebbles into the lake. The first pebble is a memorial tribute to a loved one. The second pebble expresses my gratitude for nature's wonders. The third pebble is a life-affirming vow regarding my spiritual path. Pebble-offering is a concrete expression of my thoughts and feelings.

I started making pebble offerings after I read an article on the Internet. The writer, Carolyn Scott Kortge, says that during travels she found it an easy step to go from "traveler" to "pilgrim." She writes that a few pebbles in her pocket help her make the transition. She acknowledges that sacred sites around the world inspire travelers to open their eyes to new horizons. However, she points out that the attitude of pilgrimage can be carried on any kind of trip, even a hike in a nearby woods. One need only set forth knowing that the sacred emerges where we seek it.

She quotes Gyomay Kubose, my father, from his book, *The Center Within*: "Teachings are everywhere, all around us, if only we open the mind's eye to see. Awareness of life is what makes life special. Unless we are aware, we do not learn anything. We have no inspiration and no teachings."

Indeed, if one is aware, inspiration can come from a small wildflower blooming along the path. If aware, one can receive a great teaching by seeing a maple leaf fall to the ground, showing front, showing back.

Kortge carries pebbles to affirm her desire to make every trip a journey to the sacred. She says, "Scaling the ridge of a mountain trail, or settling down to rest on the bench of a tranquil park, my hand brushes against the nuggets in my pocket, and I remember to give thanks. I drop a pebble as a gift of gratitude… My pebbles take very little space, they won't leak, spill or wilt, and don't visibly affect the place I pick from, or where I leave them later."

The offerings are simply symbols that express the spirit of the giver. The value lies not in what is given but in the intention. It is not where you go, but seeing what is around you with awareness that makes life a pilgrimage.

After reading this article, I began using pebble offerings as a mindfulness practice. I've used pebbles from my backyard, from beaches and parks, and even pebbles found along busy city sidewalks. I look at each pebble carefully before using it as an offering. I've come to realize that every pebble has its own face. Each pebble offering becomes a friendly ambassador that I send out into the world.

In my travels, I've left pebbles in many places— on the Mendenhall Glacier in Juneau, Alaska, next to a sleeping alligator in the Florida Everglades, and at the graves of friends in Greensboro, North Carolina. Here at home, I use pebble offerings on daily morning sunrise "pilgrimages" to keep my awareness fresh that each time, each sunrise, is special.

An important thing I've learned from seeing sunrises is that each sunrise is unique and should be appreciated as such. I used to have in my mind an idea of what a "perfect" sunrise was, and I would be disappointed if a sunrise didn't match my expectation. After awhile, I came to view each sunrise as absolutely unique and this enabled me to discover different aspects of each sunrise.

Sometimes clouds on the horizon look like a mountain range and the sun reflects brilliantly on the tops of the "snow-capped mountains." If the horizon is clear but there is a low-lying cloud layer overhead, when the sun goes behind these clouds, shafts of light rays can stream down like in a Renaissance painting or like a giant spaceship blasting off. Even when the sky is completely clouded over, the sunrise can be seen as a glow behind the clouds, creating a kaleidoscope of subtle shadow patterns in the gray sky.

I lead a group sunrise walk every September. We go every year, regardless of the weather. Of course, we'd prefer a beautiful, clear morning but we can also appreciate what a rainy day has to offer. In the group walks, the participants are asked to bring stones from home for their "pebble offerings." We also give each person a lit incense stick to carry while walking. As the stick gets shorter and shorter, this is a reminder of the teaching

Daybreak at Inspiration Point

of impermanence. We should appreciate each precious moment.

Whether in a group or by myself, the morning pilgrimages follow the same general routine. Yet, each sunrise is absolutely unique and will never be repeated. In the same way, my life today cannot be lived again. This present moment is not merely now but it is the eternal now. I try to view each sunrise in the eternal now of the present moment. When the sun comes up, it is a new morning, a new amazing day.

It is not an easy teaching that one should live today as today, and not as yesterday or tomorrow.

In his book *The Center Within*, my father says, "In a limited, relative sense, today is a continuation of yesterday but in reality, today is a totally new day. We live a new life every moment. Why spoil this new life? We should make this new life the best, most beautiful and most meaningful. But most of us spoil this new life because of yesterday's unpleasant affairs. Something disagreeable that happened last night still bothers us. I know some couples who do not talk to each other for two or three days. We are human, so we have these kinds of feelings. We are unable to wipe them out, unable to forget. Even if we remember to try, it is hard to forget something that has hurt us deeply. However, it is a discipline, if you want to call it discipline, wherein one is able to transcend anger and quarrels, and to start a new day. To be able to control one's own mind is to be able to live each day as a new day. This is what non-attachment means."

I remember having a hard time understanding what non-attachment meant. It does not mean detachment. It simply means not to victimize oneself by being unable to let go of one's own narrow views. Although relationships make us what we are and we have to deal with all kinds of relationships, we have to be able to "let go and grow." This is to keep the "beginner's mind." This is the meaning of "keep going."

In relationships, dichotomies arise such as superior-inferior, good-bad, right-wrong, and win-lose. "Keep going" means to go beyond such a relative world of comparisons and judgments. We do live in such a relative world but we don't have to be victimized by it. Don't stop and get stuck in such quicksand. Even if you get slowed down, keep going! Life itself is dynamic and never stops. Flow with it. This is how you can live an absolute life in a relative world. Keep going means to keep a wide perspective. Like the big sky, take in everything and keep going. The deepest meaning of "Keep Going" is infinity, which is the widest perspective possible. Make this your spiritual home.

My father continues, "Non-attachment is the basis for the fresh, creative life. Do not defile your beautiful life. That is the very reason the Buddha always referred to the lotus flower. It grows and blooms in a muddy pond but the lotus is never defiled by its environment, by the muddiness. It always keeps its own purity. When the sun comes out, the lotus opens its leaves and buds and fully appreciates the sunshine. Let us all live this kind of fresh, creative life."

Every morning the sun shines on all things without distinction. I want to live like the sun, shining brightly in the vast blue sky. May I live such a life of boundless freedom and oneness. The sun can inspire us all. I recall a poem, "The Sun Never Says," by Hafiz, a great Sufi master.

Even
After
All this time
The sun never says to the earth,

"You owe
Me."

Look
What happens
With a love like that,
It lights the
Whole
Sky.

I close my eyes and feel the sun on my face. I receive the life-giving warmth of the sun even though I have done nothing to deserve it. The sun represents all that sustains my life. I bask in nature's grace in spite of my all-too-human short-comings. I feel so blessed that I cannot help but want to give back by living a sincere, meaningful life. Since I know I am incapable of living a truly worthwhile life, I give myself over to life itself and the great flow of the universe.

As I head back to my car, I feel grateful for the sun, the lake, and for the fact that I am alive. I become mindful of my breathing. I feel relaxed but alert. I am ready to begin the day.

EPILOGUE

I hope this book can help you enrich your spiritual life. You can walk or run the route I describe and see a lakefront sunrise. This could be done by "out-of-towners" as a kind of spiritual "pilgrimage" when they visit the Chicago area. The lakefront route could be done at a non-sunrise time and still be rewarding. Just parking and watching a sunrise without going for a run or walk is also a worthwhile experience.

Yet, the purpose of my book is not limited to doing something here locally.

I hope the various aspects described in my morning ritual are like dropped "pebbles" that encourage you to look mindfully in your own daily life, no matter where you live. Consider what I have shared as an invitation for you to joyfully discover your own spiritual path. An important aspect of spirituality is a daily mindfulness practice. Teachings have to be backed by practice. Reading and listening to teachings are fine, as far as they go, but for any significant impact on your life, you must have some kind of daily spiritual practice. As a start, you are welcome to follow my lead with what I have shared in this book.

Every morning when you wash up in the bathroom, face east and welcome the new day. Do the "Toilet Gassho" with a smile. Use your dental hygiene to help nurture right speech. Thank your shoes, drive with awareness, look at the sky, at trees, and be appreciative for the wonders of nature that you take for granted every day. By taking the time to look around carefully, even ordinary things can become full of significance and mystery. By being aware, you can cultivate "spiritual karma" to provide fertile soil so that ideas and insights, like seeds, can send down roots to nourish and anchor your spirituality.

The process of spiritual growth can be likened to the gradual beneficial effects of daily habits, like brushing teeth and taking vitamins, that are done for physical health. The effects of a daily spiritual practice are gradual, cumulative and not necessarily dramatic. Always maintain a Wide View of things. Just begin the process and Keep Going. As it has been said, "Thoughts become actions, which become habits, which become character, which become destiny."

The continuity of a daily spiritual practice can be likened to a long telephone wire that stretches across the countryside. Retreats and special events are like telephone poles that at occasional intervals elevate and hold up the wire. An individual daily practice and activities done in a group setting complement and support each other.

Saying grace before meals is a common example of how a spiritual practice is linked to an everyday activity. The kinds of mindfulness practices I describe are examples of other ways to extend the idea of integrating spirituality into everyday activities.

Discovering such mindfulness practices is a creative process that is rewarding and relevant because the discoveries come out of one's own personal life. As you discover and accumulate various practices, you do not necessarily need to do all of them every single day. I like to think of the practices as being added to one's "spiritual tool bag" and just like pliers and screwdrivers, they can come in handy when situations arise in one's daily life.

I would enjoy hearing about any innovative practices you discover for yourself and add to your own "spiritual tool bag." May we all widen and deepen our everyday spirituality and thus promote peace within and harmony with others.

In Oneness,
S. K. Kubose

MAP

Bright Dawn

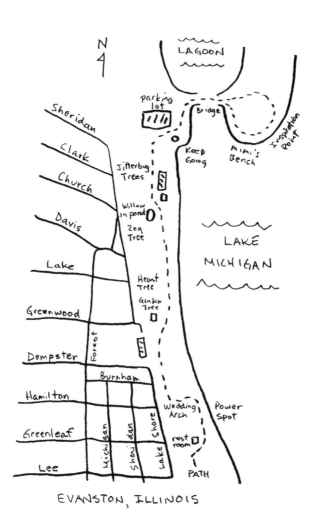

EVANSTON, ILLINOIS

Bright Dawn

ADDITIONAL INFORMATION

For Your Spiritual Journey
from the
Kubose Dharma Legacy

Universal teachings for everyday living is the focus of the "Way of Oneness" approach of the late Rev. Gyomay M. Kubose, who was a pioneer in the Americanization of Buddhism. His approach emphasizes Oneness, the non-dualistic reality of life beyond all conceptual labels. Starting from his training as a Shin Buddhist priest in the Japanese Mahayana tradition, he developed an eclectic approach that drew freely from the original teachings of the historical Gautama Buddha, from Zen Buddhism, and other Buddhist schools.

In his own words, "I have always dreamed of establishing an American Buddhism—different from Indian, Chinese, or Japanese Buddhism—a uniquely American Buddhism that could be easily understood and practiced by Americans and that would contribute to American life and culture. This Buddhism can be described in simple, everyday language and practiced in all aspects of daily life. Yet, it is a unique Buddhist life-way, non-dichotomized and non-dualistic, that will bring about a peaceful, meaningful, creative life, both individually and collectively."

The "Way of Oneness" approach puts the focus on individual spiritual growth rather than on any particular sectarian dogma. The interest is not in converting people to an "ism" with the label of Buddhism. Universal teachings for everyday living can be used by people of any religious background. It has been said that Buddhism always gives, never takes away. It would be wonderful if the teachings could help a Christian become a better Christian, a Jew become a better Jew, a Muslim become a better Muslim, or even an atheist become a better atheist. Individual spirituality is beyond religious labels.

Rev. Koyo Kubose is carrying on his father's Way of Oneness approach. A nonprofit educational organization has been established, which distributes books, sponsors seminars and classes, and offers additional resources that can support and encourage individual spirituality.

A free videotape loan program is available for individual or group use. The videos are of innovative American Buddhist services held in Evanston, Illinois by Heartland Sangha (www.heartlandsangha.org). Each service is uniquely planned by a volunteer chairperson. Music and readings are used from a variety of sources. Gratitude and nourishment offerings of flowers or rice grains replace traditional incense offering and sutra chanting. Rev. Koyo Kubose's Dharma talks are always lively and humorous due to his down-to-earth speaking style.

You are welcome to call "Dial-the-Dharma" (847-677-8053) to hear a one-minute taped talk. This unique 24-hour telephone service, with tapes changed daily, comes from a library of 365 talks by Revs. Gyomay and Koyo Kubose.

There is no subscription fee to receive a quarterly newsletter, "Oneness," to stay informed of new books and programs. To be put on the mailing list, visit the website: www.brightdawn.org.

Bright Dawn

THE AUTHOR

Sunnan Koyo Kubose was born in Los Angeles. He went with his family to World War II camps in Heart Moutain, Wyoming and Poston, Arizona. His family relocated to Chicago, where he attended elementary and high school. He went to college at the University of California at Berkeley and then continued with postgraduate work, earning an M.A. from San Francisco State University, and a Ph.D. in psychology from the

University of Iowa. He has been on the faculties at the University of North Carolina at Greensboro, University of Hawaii, and University of Wisconsin Center System. He went to Japan for three years, and studied Shin Buddhism at the Eastern Buddhist Society at Otani University. He also did meditation with Zen masters Uchiyama Kosho of the Soto tradition and Kobori Nanrei of the Rinzai tradition.

Rev. Koyo Kubose served on the ministerial staff at the Buddhist Temple of Chicago from 1983 to 1995 to work with his father in creatively developing Buddhism in America. He served as the Executive Director of the Japanese American Service Committee from 1995 to 1996. From 1997 on, he has worked towards establishing the Rev. Gyomay M. Kubose Dharma Legacy as an educational organization dedicated to carrying on his father's lifework.

"BRIGHT DAWN" BOOK ORDERING INFORMATION

Order Direct From Publisher with option for autographed copy:

Complete order form below and send with payment to:

   Dharma House, 8334 Harding Avenue, Skokie, IL 60076.

Price: US $12.95 each
Sales Tax: 8.5% for books shipped to Illinois.
                (US $1.10 per book)
Shipping: US $3.95 for the first book and US $1.45 for each
                additional book. For shipping rates outside the
                USA, call (847) 677-8211.
Payments: Money order or checks made payable to:
                Dharma House

Price	Quantity	Total
US $12.95 X	_____	_____

8.5% IL sales tax, if applicable   _____

Shipping & Handling   _____

Total Enclosed   _____

Name: _____

Address: _____

_____

Autographed by Author?   YES   NO